I0459586

God Moments

Volume 2

30 Daily Devotions
to Awaken and Grow Your Faith

WENDY ADDISON

OLDE CROW PUBLISHING

God Moments – Volume 2
30 Daily Devotions to Awaken and Grow Your Faith

© 2025 by Wendy Addison

Scripture quotations marked (ESV) are from The ESV® Bible (The Holy Bible, English Standard Version®), © 2001 by Crossway, a publishing ministry of Good News Publishers. Used by permission. All rights reserved

Scripture quotations marked (NASB) are taken from the (NASB®) New American Standard Bible®, Copyright © 1960, 1971, 1977, 1995, 2020 by The Lockman Foundation. Used by permission. All rights reserved. www.lockman.org

Scripture quotations marked (NIV) are taken from the Holy Bible, New International Version®, NIV®. Copyright © 1973, 1978, 1984, 2011 by Biblica, Inc.™ Used by permission of Zondervan. All rights reserved worldwide. www.zondervan.com The "NIV" and "New International Version" are trademarks registered in the United States Patent and Trademark Office by Biblica, Inc.™

Scripture quotations marked (NLT) are taken from the *Holy Bible*, New Living Translation, copyright ©1996, 2004, 2015 by Tyndale House Foundation. Used by permission of Tyndale House Publishers, Carol Stream, Illinois 60188. All rights reserved.

Published in Ontario, Canada by Olde Crow Publishing.

ISBN: 978-1-990081-14-9 (paperback edition)
ISBN: 978-1-990081-13-2 (e-book)

2. Every chapter stands on its own. However, when put together as a whole, they describe as much of the rideshare driving experience as I can put into words.

3. The stories are all true, but I'm not here to ruin lives. With that in mind, I've gone out of my way to ensure each story's characters can't be attached to the people involved. The locations in my stories are real, but I've removed or changed identifying information of individual riders. For flow and clarity I've named many passengers, but none are their actual names. I've also detailed situations and descriptions of characters that are true to the story, but modified enough to keep passengers' identities safe. Unless you were in the car, you don't know who it is. If by some chance you think you know who I'm talking about, you don't—unless it's you.

4. I'm sure that the rideshare companies would dispute some of the things I say about them and the conclusions I draw about their business practices. Full disclosure: I'm not privy to their internal conversations and the intent behind their decisions. As a result, I can't speak with certainty about their motivations. I can, however, discuss how their decisions impact the drivers and passengers using their platform. I can also state that everything I say about them has happened to me or a fellow driver with whom I've spoken or has been printed or published in articles, stories, and books describing their history and business practices.

Now, let's get to the good stuff.

they want is to embed their product into your life until it becomes indispensable. Once that happens, the company is positioned to crush their competition and increase profits.

The two major rideshare companies, Lyft and Uber, are the same way. Both are ruthless, cutthroat companies with little concern for making the world better. Everything they do is designed to increase profits. They have whole departments dedicated to fine-tuning and strategizing how to use psychology and AI to exploit both passengers and drivers.

Enough about that for now. You may wonder how my side hustle turned into a book. When I started driving, I had no idea what I would see, hear, and experience. More than once, I had to park my car after a ride and ask myself whether something a passenger did really happened. To process these experiences, I vented on social media under the hashtag #UberProTips. These posts were generally well received, and every time I posted, at least one person encouraged me to write a book. As I continued to drive and the stories became more and more outrageous, I realized those people suggesting a book were onto something.

While it's impossible to describe all I encountered over my years giving 10,000 rides, I hope the following stories give some idea what it was like.

Before we begin, a few disclaimers.

1. Instead of telling the story chronologically, I've organized them from A to Z like an encyclopedia. (Remember those?) The chapters switch topics and aren't required to be read in order. Scan the table of contents, find a title that catches your attention, and read.

Reflections

What spoke to you the most from today's reading?

_____

_____

_____

_____

Turn your thoughts into a prayer:

_____

_____

_____

_____

Is the Holy Spirit prompting you to do anything in response?

_____

_____

_____

_____

sure - but it's only for a time. We all need to grow and move on to the next thing.

> *So let us stop going over the basic*
> *teachings about Christ again and again.*
> *Let us go on instead and become*
> *mature in our understanding.*
> *(Hebrews 6:1 – NLT)*

Are you hanging out in a nest that is no longer fit for your size? How can you grow deeper in your relationship with God this week?

Day 6

One spring, after spending time at the river, my daughter came home eager to share a story with her bird-loving mom.

Sitting near an osprey nest, she watched a mama osprey coax her baby to fly.

The fearful baby osprey flapped his wings and called to its mom, teetering on the edge of the nest but not daring to leap from it.

So, what did the mama do? She caught a fish and darted back and forth in front of the baby, keeping the fish just out of reach.

Eventually, the baby was encouraged enough to leap from the safety of its nest and find new freedom in the sky (and dinner).

Oh, how I wish I'd been there to see it!

Because, again, as so many things in nature do, it reminds me of God's love.

He doesn't force us to go in the direction He wants. He waits for us. Encourages us.

Shows us the good He has for us if we follow Him.

Staying in the nest isn't good. It's comfortable,

Reflections

What spoke to you the most from today's reading?

_____

_____

_____

_____

Turn your thoughts into a prayer:

_____

_____

_____

_____

Is the Holy Spirit prompting you to do anything in response?

_____

_____

_____

_____

But here's what I DO know. God is truth. His word, His promises, His love. All those are true.

Jesus said to him, "I am the way,and the truth, and the life. No one comes to the Father except through me."
(John 14:6 – ESV)

All Scripture is breathed out by God and profitable for teaching, for reproof, for correction, and for training in righteousness.
(2 Timothy 3:16 – ESV)

Are you ill? God's Word is true.

Are you in a war zone? God's promises hold true.

Does life seem hopeless? God is truth, and He is here.

So, remember, when all seems lost, hopeless, and confusing, we can always turn to the One who is always true and steadfast.

Lean on Him. He will always remain.

Day 5

We live in an age when we can see what's happening across the globe in the blink of an eye. It's incredible to be so interconnected.

But equally, it's also easy for anyone to say anything and for opinions to look like facts.

I mean, really - I could probably fabricate a story about Russia attacking Ukraine to hide evidence of aliens. I could look up a few references linking Area 51, mark up a few maps, photoshop a few photos, and throw in a few quotes from 'experts' in the field, fabricated or not. And if I did it professionally enough, I'm sure some people would believe it.

So, what is real in light of everything happening in today's world? We know we can't always trust the news, so who do we believe?

In every issue, some people say one thing, and some say another. Fake photos circulate the internet along with real ones. But which photos are real? What is the truth? Is it a conspiracy theory? Or is it true? In reality, I don't know which news is real or fake. I have my ideas, but nothing I can fully present as fact.

Reflections

What spoke to you the most from today's reading?

_____

_____

_____

_____

Turn your thoughts into a prayer:

_____

_____

_____

_____

Is the Holy Spirit prompting you to do anything in response?

_____

_____

_____

_____

kind of day, this was it.

Yet, I still felt like I was doing what God wanted me to, and I was reaching out to Him all day long.

So, what was up?

First, God never promises to make our days perfect. But if you continually seek Him, He promises peace amidst the chaos.

Second, I pressed on. I kept going.

And it paid off.

I borrowed another wheelbarrow and got the job done. The website eventually uploaded my book info, and the other website did, too. Everything else also worked out.

Commit everything you do to the Lord.
Trust him, and he will help you.
(Psalm 37:5 – NLT)

Perhaps it was a lesson in perseverance? Or maybe it was just about trusting God in all circumstances.

Ultimately, I encourage you to keep seeking Him, no matter what. He is there with you.

You are not alone in your struggles.

Day 4

Normally, I can tell the difference between days when I continually seek God to order my day and days when I try to do it myself.

Generally, the God-led day is peaceful. Things flow better, and I usually get more done.

When I barge ahead, do what I 'need' to do, and leave God out of it, I'm often met with frustration, impatience, and overwhelm.

But, one day, it proved to be a little different.

It was a God-led day, but everything still kept going wrong.

I'd lined everything up for a yard project, only to find out the wheelbarrow tire was flat and unfixable.

I ran into multiple problems trying to upload books to a platform. I spent a long time entering information, only to have the site crash just before I finished. This happened more than five times.

So, I moved on to something else. Then that site crashed, too.

These are only three examples of many in my chaotic day. If you've ever heard of a Murphy's Law

Reflections

What spoke to you the most from today's reading?

_____

_____

_____

_____

Turn your thoughts into a prayer:

_____

_____

_____

_____

Is the Holy Spirit prompting you to do anything in response?

_____

_____

_____

_____

Look at the birds of the air; they do not sow or reap or store away in barns, and yet your heavenly Father feeds them. Are you not much more valuable than they?
(Matthew 6:26 – NIV)

And yes, my friends. We are more valuable than they. The next verse, 6:27, says,

Can any one of you by worrying add a single hour to your life?

We all know the answer to this is a big, fat, "No!"

So, why do we worry? Why do I give in Every. Single. Day. And let the troubles of this world overcome me rather than trusting in our amazing, powerful God, day by day?

If I ever figure it out, I'll let you know.

In the meantime, I'll do my best to continually turn over my cares to Him. Again. And again. And again. And I encourage you to do the same.

Don't give up! Keep trusting Him.

Day 3

I love having the bird feeders outside my office window. It is great to see so many of my feathered friends return home after the cold, harsh winter.

And that got me thinking... how on earth do these little fluffy birdies possibly fly all the way south and then back up to my little backyard in Canada every year?

How do they *find* it?

I mean, I've driven to Florida. It's *far* from Ontario. I can't imagine flying there with little wings, let alone finding where I need to go without a map or a GPS!

And yet, they do it.

Every year.

And God provides for them. They don't worry about where to stop for dinner. They don't worry about tomorrow's weather or how they will possibly complete the daunting task ahead of them.

It's like there's a sacred trust between them and God.

Reflections

What spoke to you the most from today's reading?

_____

_____

_____

_____

Turn your thoughts into a prayer:

_____

_____

_____

_____

Is the Holy Spirit prompting you to do anything in response?

_____

_____

_____

_____

We're Marthas when we should be Marys.

We miss the mark.

How many times a week - or even a day - do we flail about on our own when God is right there asking us to spend time with Him? To come to Him, to rest with Him?

How often do we settle for our own methods instead of asking for His help?

Teach me your way, Lord, that I may rely on your faithfulness; give me an undivided heart, that I may fear your name.
(Psalm 86:11– NIV)

So, that's today's advice - don't miss the mark.

Sleep in the cat bed.

And, for the record, the cats did eventually settle into their new beds. Cat treats and catnip may or may not have been involved.

Day 2

Have you ever felt like you've missed the mark?

When I still had only three cats, I bought a cat bed – *one* bed. I didn't think it would be an issue since only one of the three seemed to be a cat-bed type of feline.

Yet, as we know, cats have minds of their own. Two cats liked the bed. One is a bully and decided to kick the other out whenever he wanted a turn.

So, what does a good cat mom do? Buy another bed, of course. And not just one more, because we can't have the third cat be bedless while the other two have theirs, can we?

Nope. I bought two more.

My purchases arrived, and I opened them with excitement and anticipation - like a mom with a surprise for her children (because - yup, that's what it is).

And guess what? Two beds lay vacant while two cats curled up *beside* the beds on a blanket.

Isn't that just typical? Silly cats.

Yet, aren't we the same? We settle for the 'okay' thing when the better thing is right in front of us.

Reflections

What spoke to you the most from today's reading?

_____

_____

_____

_____

Turn your thoughts into a prayer:

_____

_____

_____

_____

Is the Holy Spirit prompting you to do anything in response?

_____

_____

_____

_____

Do you remember what Jesus said to Martha in Luke?

"Martha, Martha," the Lord answered, "you are worried and upset about many things, but few things are needed—or indeed only one. Mary has chosen what is better, and it will not be taken away from her."
(Luke 10:41-42 – NIV)

Yes, there are chores that need to be done. Yes, there are children who need tending to. And yes, there are errands to run.

But, above all, God wants us to sit with Him. To focus on Him.

If we don't have time for that, does anything else we do really matter?

And interestingly, the days I put God first and spend time with Him are the days when everything else usually falls into place.

Will you trust Him with your time today?

Day 1

No matter the season, our time is in demand, and we get busy. In the fall, school starts, and groups, clubs, and activities reconvene. In winter, some of that dies down, but activities are just replaced with indoor events rather than outdoor ones.

By the time summer comes around, it feels like it should be vacation time, but the summer months easily fill up, too. I may have a break from homeschooling, but then the time gets filled with camping trips, gardening, homesteading, reading, planning, and driving kids around.

No matter the time of year, it can be non-stop, go, go, go.

I often wonder where the time will come from to complete everything on my list, but I'm a natural multitasker, which helps.

Or does it?

I'm reminded of the story of Mary and Martha entertaining Jesus at their home. Martha rushed around preparing food and doing hostess duties, while Mary just sat at Jesus' feet and listened to Him.

connection with the day's message. Take a moment to breathe deeply and immerse yourself in this exercise. God has incredible things to reveal to you. But if you're uncertain you're truly hearing His voice, always align it with scripture. God's Word is a steadfast guide, and through practice, persistence, and prayer, you will grow attuned to the Holy Spirit.

Remember, God desires a close and personal relationship with you. He loves you deeply and calls you His own. Don't lose heart; keep seeking, and let this devotional journey draw you nearer to His presence.

Wendy.

Introduction

Welcome to volume two of my *God Moments* devotional series. I'm thrilled to share these devotions with you in book format!

Thanks to your heartfelt feedback, what began as a devotional section in my author newsletter has evolved into something much more meaningful. Many of you shared how these messages have enriched and challenged your faith, and your requests for a book have inspired this series.

I invite you to pause and deeply engage with the scriptures and reflections in each devotion. These are not meant to be just another item to check off your to-do list but rather an opportunity to slow down, assess your faith, and deepen your relationship with Jesus. My prayer is that these moments will inspire spiritual growth and more intimacy with God.

At the end of each devotion, you'll find questions designed to prompt reflection and

Volume 2

And aren't we like that? We come into this world all squeaky clean and new.

And then we crack.

We slip up. We make mistakes. We sin.

But here's the good news!

Therefore, if anyone is in Christ,
the new creation has come:
The old has gone, the new is here!
(2 Corinthians 5:17 – NIV)

When we turn to God, repent of our sins, and follow Jesus, He makes all things new - forever!

God doesn't see the cracks when he looks at us (or the vast smashed-up parts, as it may be). And that is good news. Rejoice, my friends!

Day 7

When my second daughter was about sixteen, she broke her phone and used her boyfriend's tablet for six months instead.

But she missed having a phone number. And frankly, I missed it, too! What did parents do before phones when they needed to reach their kids?

I mean, I remember using a pay phone to call my parents when I was in school, but how did they reach me? (And yes, I am regularly-used-a-payphone years old.) They must have left messages at the office or something. Or just waited until I got home from school.

So, she got a new phone, and it was nice to reach her easily again.

And then she went away on the weekend. All was good until I received a frantic text - she dropped the phone and broke it! Already!

To be fair, I don't think it was entirely her fault. But still, she's justifiably upset. Thankfully, the only damage sustained was a few small cracks, and she could live with them. But I understood her disappointment.

Reflections

What spoke to you the most from today's reading?

_____

_____

_____

_____

Turn your thoughts into a prayer:

_____

_____

_____

_____

Is the Holy Spirit prompting you to do anything in response?

_____

_____

_____

_____

Day 8

I love walking after a snowfall. Everything seems fresh and new, and I love how the snow sparkles as it rests on the tree branches.

Something else that stands out is the fresh footprints all along my trail through the woods – cute red squirrel prints ending at the base of a tree, a zigzagging mouse trail, and similar prints spaced farther apart, left by someone in a hurry.

The neighbour's big, orange barn cat usually leaves a trail or two, as do rabbits, birds, and the occasional fox.

The amount of wildlife present in my woods astounds me.

Except, other than for the footprints, I might never know they were there. Don't get me wrong; I do occasionally see wildlife in my woods, but for the most part, the animals are quiet and elusive.

But they're there.

And so is God.

Where shall I go from your Spirit? Or where shall I flee from your presence? If I ascend to heaven, you are there! If I make my bed in Sheol, you are there! If I take the wings of the morning and dwell in the uttermost parts of the sea, even there your hand shall lead me, and your right hand shall hold me.
(Psalm 139:7-10 – ESV)

Looking with the right eyes, I can see evidence of Him everywhere. But if I don't pay attention, I might miss it. Either way, the fact remains the same—He is always there with me and with you—walking with us, looking over us, listening to our prayers and worship, and enveloping us with His presence.

Nothing can separate us from His love when we are His children.

Reflections

What spoke to you the most from today's reading?

_____

_____

_____

_____

Turn your thoughts into a prayer:

_____

_____

_____

_____

Is the Holy Spirit prompting you to do anything in response?

_____

_____

_____

_____

Day 9

Sometimes, I go through cycles where I get really tired. And by tired, I mean completely exhausted.

A combination of things in my life sometimes emotionally drain me to the point where I hit a wall, and instead of making healthy choices, I enter into a vicious cycle: I feel tired, eat sugar, and wake up at night from too much sugar (and the stress). And the next day, I feel tired, eat sugar, and repeat.

I find myself once again turning to something else to feed me other than looking to God for rest and peace.

Give all your worries and cares to God,
for he cares about you.
(1 Peter 5:7 – NLT).

Note that Peter doesn't tell us to, "Eat sugar (or use caffeine) to get through your day".

For everything there is a season,
a time for every activity under heaven.
(Ecclesiastes 3:1 – NLT)

Most of us are familiar with the string of verses in Ecclesiastes about a "time to dance, and a time to mourn..." and the others that follow.

But nowhere in there does it say, "a time to worry, a time to stress eat, a time to drink wine to forget, or a time to try and fix it all yourself."

Are there things in life weighing you down? Will you join me today in giving our worries to God?

He's always there, waiting for you.

He wants to ease your burden.

Reflections

What spoke to you the most from today's reading?

_____

_____

_____

_____

Turn your thoughts into a prayer:

_____

_____

_____

_____

Is the Holy Spirit prompting you to do anything in response?

_____

_____

_____

_____

Day 10

If there's one consistent thing, it's that things are always changing.

I'm excited that autumn is here, but soon, snow will fall. And then melt. And then it will get hot again, followed by another autumn. That might sound consistent, yet it's not. We never know what each season will bring.

Will the winter be mild? Or will there be an onslaught of snowstorms? Will the summer be too wet or too dry? Or a perfect balance of rain and sun with the best growing season ever?

What about tornadoes and hurricanes? Or surprise beautiful days and extra sunshine?

And just like the weather, so is life.

Are you going through a storm of your own right now? Did you recently experience the death of a loved one? A sickness? The end of a close relationship?

Or perhaps you're in a blessed season, with good health, a satisfying career, enjoying mended friendships, family births, and new marriages.

I know the Lord is always with me.
I will not be shaken, for
He is right beside me.
(Psalm 16:8 – NLT)

No matter what season you're in, there is one thing that never changes.

God.

He is always with you. He is our Rock. He is our solid fortress.

Feeling weary? Bring Him your burdens and rest in His love. In a season of plenty? Share His blessings with others He puts in your path.

And in every season, praise His goodness and Holiness.

He is always with you.

Reflections

What spoke to you the most from today's reading?

_____

_____

_____

_____

Turn your thoughts into a prayer:

_____

_____

_____

_____

Is the Holy Spirit prompting you to do anything in response?

_____

_____

_____

_____

Day 11

One morning, I woke up to the overwhelming, cackling chorus of a plague of migrating grackles. They'd decided to rest in my backyard and forage for breakfast.

Without hesitation, I hopped out of bed and went outside.

I walked the trail around the edge of the property. There must have been thousands of them! And they were loud.

It was wonderful.

You see, one of the ways I worship God is through birdwatching. There are so many unique avian species, each with intricate characteristics and extraordinary abilities.

Like the killdeer who feigns a broken wing to lure predators away from her nest of young ones.

Or the yellow-bellied sapsucker, whose long tongue wraps around inside its head when not in use.

And the cedar waxwings who pass berries down the line from beak to beak.

Spending time outdoors draws me closer to

God. It reminds me of His creativity and floods my soul with His peace.

I have friends who feel this way when they sing a song. Their voices are angelic, and singing to the Lord makes them feel close to Him.

I have other friends who are artists. Their paintings come alive with emotions and feelings as they portray the landscapes God created.

And, of course, my gardener friends feel closest to God when they dig their hands into the warm soil and watch how He creates plants and food from seeds.

Let everything that has breath
praise the Lord. (Psalm 150:6 – NIV)

So, how do you worship God, my friend? What is it you do to feel close to Him? What draws you into his presence?

And more importantly, are you spending time worshiping Him that way?

The world seems more chaotic than ever these days. Take a moment today to revel in Jesus's love. Breathe in His peace and goodness. Breathe out praise and thanksgiving.

Reflections

What spoke to you the most from today's reading?

_____

_____

_____

_____

Turn your thoughts into a prayer:

_____

_____

_____

_____

Is the Holy Spirit prompting you to do anything in response?

_____

_____

_____

_____

Day 12

Usually, when I write the God Moment for my newsletter, I already know the week's event I will share and use to make a Biblical parallel.

But one particular week, I didn't have one. I prayed, and thought, prayed and thought, but nothing came to mind.

And then it occurred to me. Do you ever feel like God isn't there? Do you ever feel like He's distant or uninvolved in your life?

Let me assure you, He's not distant. He's close.

Very close.

And just because you don't feel Him or see how He's working, it doesn't mean He isn't there.

He's always working. He's always present. And if you have repented of your sins, asked Jesus to forgive you, and decided to follow Him, then God's even closer than you can imagine.

He's in your heart.

The Holy Spirit lives in us.

And if you haven't asked, what are you waiting for?

You will seek me and find me, when you seek me with all your heart.
(Jeremiah 29:13 – ESV)

I've personally experienced this.

And remember - it's not all about feelings. It's about faith.

Believing. And knowing.

So, if He feels distant today, let me encourage you to spend time with Him. Believe He is there. Know He is with you. Trust in Him. He loves you.

Reflections

What spoke to you the most from today's reading?

_____

_____

_____

_____

Turn your thoughts into a prayer:

_____

_____

_____

_____

Is the Holy Spirit prompting you to do anything in response?

_____

_____

_____

_____

Day 13

One of the things I look forward to in the fall is getting back to schedules and routines. I'm an organizer and a planner, so yes, I get excited by these things!

Yet, at the same time, it can also be a bit overwhelming. My calendar gets full very quickly. Add some regular 'life' stuff to that, and it suddenly feels like every minute is crammed with tasks or activities.

So, what do you do when life takes over? He says:

Be still, and know that I am God.
(Psalm 46:10 – NIV)

I've quoted this verse a few times in various God Moments because it deserves multiple shares and because I need to hear it over and over, too.

Is life too busy?

Be still, and know that I am God.

Are you overwhelmed?

Be still, and know that I am God.

Going through tragic circumstances?

Be still, and know that I am God.

Struggling with sickness?

Be still.

Worried about war around the world?

Know that I am God.

No matter how many things are squished into our calendars or what we're going through that commands our thoughts, it's essential to make time to sit with Him. Not just when you have time, not when you think you'll get to it, but now. In fact, it's the most important thing.

Everything else will wait.

Be still, my friend.

Know that HE IS GOD.

Reflections

What spoke to you the most from today's reading?

_____

_____

_____

_____

Turn your thoughts into a prayer:

_____

_____

_____

_____

Is the Holy Spirit prompting you to do anything in response?

_____

_____

_____

_____

Day 14

Press on. Run the race. Don't give up.

Do those words resonate with you?

I was surprised to see how many times in the New Testament, Paul compares the Christian faith to running a race. That kind of stinks because, trust me, you don't want to see me jogging, let alone running! I'm glad it's all for the sake of a metaphor.

Do you not know that in a race all the runners run, but only one gets the prize? Run in such a way as to get the prize. Everyone who competes in the games goes into strict training. They do it to get a crown that will not last, but we do it to get a crown that will last forever. Therefore I do not run like someone running aimlessly; I do not fight like a boxer beating the air. No, I strike a blow to my body and make it my slave so that after I have preached to others, I myself will not be disqualified for the prize. (1 Corinthians 9:24-27 – NIV)

But the words ring true. Reading all the references together paints a bigger picture.

Press on. Hold on to what is good. Keep your eyes on Him. And don't just run to finish the race; run to win.

Is there something pressing on your heart that you know God wants you to be doing? Are you giving Him your all? Are you obeying His call on your life? Let me encourage you to answer Him and run into His arms at full speed, letting nothing else get in the way.

Nothing compares to living your life like this.

Remember, if you ever feel derailed, our God is a forgiving God. His love and mercy are always there to guide you back on track. So, don't lose heart, and keep pressing on in your faith.

Reflections

What spoke to you the most from today's reading?

_____

_____

_____

_____

Turn your thoughts into a prayer:

_____

_____

_____

_____

Is the Holy Spirit prompting you to do anything in response?

_____

_____

_____

_____

Day 15

One morning, while homeschooling my youngest, I noticed something interesting.

All I have to say is, "Let's do math now," and the sweet princess of a girl instantly turns into a fuming ogre.

I mean, we haven't even pulled out the books yet, and her shoulders are already hunched up, and her eyes are glazed over.

I think, in today's language, you would say math is a "trigger" for her.

There's no reason for it to be. It's not her strong suit, but she's completely capable and good at learning the equations.

Let me be clear. The problem is not the math itself but a prior wounding. Somewhere in her past, she felt dumb, inadequate, or unworthy while doing math (maybe more than once). And the pain resurfaces the second I say the word.

Then she becomes instantly defensive and less receptive to learning, and handling life at that moment.

And don't we all have triggers of some sort?

For me, it's feeling like I disappointed someone I love. Or feeling like I'm not good enough.

And just like my daughter with math, those things are often not true, but feelings resurface from my past when triggered.

Do not conform to the pattern
of this world, but be transformed
by the renewing of your mind.
(Romans 12:2 – NIV)

If I could see it from the outside looking in, maybe I could change my reaction and handle things better.

Instead of resorting to old feelings by habit, perhaps I could lean on the One Who Makes All Things New and let Him heal my wounds instead of letting the wounds control me.

So, whether your trigger is math or a more profound wound from your past, let Him renew your mind. He can, and will, make all things new.

Reflections

What spoke to you the most from today's reading?

_____

_____

_____

_____

Turn your thoughts into a prayer:

_____

_____

_____

_____

Is the Holy Spirit prompting you to do anything in response?

_____

_____

_____

_____

Day 16

On one of my daily walks, a certain tree caught my eye. It was dead, the bark fallen off in a heap on the ground. But what stood out was the intricate etchings in the tree—swirls, lines, and amazing little patterns.

I don't know for certain, but based on my internet searches and the fact that we have ash trees on our property, I'm sure the designs were damage caused by an emerald ash borer. These little beetles have attacked most of the ash trees in our area of Ontario, and not many trees have survived.

Yet, they've created a work of art through their damage!

Don't get me wrong - I'm not happy about all the trees getting destroyed - but it's rather interesting to see literal 'beauty from ashes.'

It got me thinking. How many of us have been damaged by sin? Either our own sin or other people's sin directed at us? None of us are immune to it. We are all hurt, broken, and weary.

Therefore, if anyone is in Christ,
he is a new creation. The old has passed
away; behold, the new has come.
(2 Corinthians 5:17 – ESV)

Yet with God, through His Son Jesus Christ, we have hope. We are renewed, restored, and rejuvenated.

He will never fail to bring beauty out of ashes.

Look to Him the next time you feel dejected. Look to Him when you need hope. Look to Him in all things.

He's waiting for you.

Reflections

What spoke to you the most from today's reading?

_____

_____

_____

_____

Turn your thoughts into a prayer:

_____

_____

_____

_____

Is the Holy Spirit prompting you to do anything in response?

_____

_____

_____

_____

Day 17

When one of my best friends lost her father, my heart was heavy, and everything else I was thinking about before the moment I found out suddenly seemed so trivial.

Like how awful I felt the week before with my 'bad cold.'

Or how the weather was too hot.

Or the difficulties I had writing, or working, or... I think you know what I mean.

I'm sure we've all been in a situation where we see how life can change in the blink of an eye.

Yet, we so rarely live that way.

I have goals and dreams, most of them fairly specific, and I don't think there's anything wrong with that.

Many are the plans in the mind
of a man, but it is the purpose
of the Lord that will stand.
(Proverbs 19:21 – ESV)

So go ahead and make plans, live life, and do your best.

But know that God is the one in control. Not me, not you. GOD.

And when life throws us for a loop, and the unexpected comes, it's okay to be sad, angry, or disappointed. It's okay to question Him and wonder why things happen as they do.

Feel your emotions, but then be still and know that He is there with you. He's got you. He'll see you through.

Always.

Reflections

What spoke to you the most from today's reading?

_____

_____

_____

_____

Turn your thoughts into a prayer:

_____

_____

_____

_____

Is the Holy Spirit prompting you to do anything in response?

_____

_____

_____

_____

Day 18

I once went to a doctor who took some of my blood and put it under a microscope.

Apparently, red blood cells are supposed to be nice, even circles that touch each other. Kind of like a waffle (except circles, not squares).

Mine looked more like a two-year-old's wall scribbling. And there might have been the odd McDonald's French fry floating in there, too.

The biggest reason mine looked like that was because I wasn't drinking enough water. Each cell has a water membrane that helps it bounce off the others and not overlap. Mine didn't have that so they kind of just squashed together.

I never 'felt' thirsty, though. And I did drink water, just not a lot.

So, I drank my full eight cups daily for the next ten days. And I did feel a difference. I had more energy, slept better, and experienced a decrease in appetite.

Isn't our walk with God like that? We do all the things, and don't feel like we need more. We go to church, pray, read our Bibles—and isn't that enough?

But there is more.

So much more.

We can immerse ourselves in Him. Drink from the Word and His presence all day long.

And what a difference there is in us when we do!

Remember the story of the Samaritan woman at the well?

Jesus answered her, "If you knew the gift of God, and who it is that is saying to you, 'Give me a drink,' you would have asked him, and he would have given you living water."
(John 4:10 – ESV)

Won't you join me today in drinking from the living water?

Reflections

What spoke to you the most from today's reading?

_____

_____

_____

_____

Turn your thoughts into a prayer:

_____

_____

_____

_____

Is the Holy Spirit prompting you to do anything in response?

_____

_____

_____

_____

Day 19

One of my favourite things to do is to walk around a campground at night. I love the crackling fires, the laughter amongst close family and friends, and the night sounds of birds and insects. It's peaceful and soothing.

The campground I go to has two separate camping areas, joined by a beach and a short woodsy trail. One night, I wasn't ready to return to our site after walking the usual loop, so I headed to the beach to also walk the other one. But, by the time I got around it and back to the crossing point, it was pitch black.

Most of the time, I walk without a flashlight. The campfires give enough light to see the roadway; however, when I arrived at where the cross trail should be, I realized I'd walked too far.

I turned on my flashlight and saw the trail a few feet behind me, so I turned around and followed it. But a few minutes in, I realized I was on the wrong trail. This trail went deep in the forest to the amphitheatre.

There I was, in the middle of the dark woods,

with only a tiny flashlight. Did I mention there are large coyotes in Ontario?

Suddenly, it didn't feel so peaceful.

I picked up my pace to get to the next cross trail and out of the woods. I made it out alive, but it was pretty creepy!

And isn't life like that?

If we aren't following God – the true light – it's easy to get sidetracked and end up on the wrong path.

It can lead us to places we don't want to go.

Your word is a lamp to my feet
And a light to my path.
(Psalm 119:105 – ESV)

But rest assured, He will always lead us out of those places if we follow the Light again. God will guide us back to Him. And He will teach us through the Bible – His Word.

Reflections

What spoke to you the most from today's reading?

_____

_____

_____

_____

Turn your thoughts into a prayer:

_____

_____

_____

_____

Is the Holy Spirit prompting you to do anything in response?

_____

_____

_____

_____

Day 20

Along with all the lovely things of autumn come a few little brown-nosed, black-eyed, big-eared mousy things seeking shelter from winter – a decision they quickly regret when they realize four cats live here.

Usually, we rescue the critters before they get hurt, and give them a nice new home in the woodshed. But once, I freed a mouse whose chest was heaving up and down in rapid breaths and one of his tiny legs stuck out at an awkward angle.

Still, my daughter brought it out to the shed in hopes that it might survive the cold night. She even provided a warm sock for the little guy to help keep him warm.

First thing the next morning, she ran to the shed to check on him. Unfortunately, he didn't make it. This made her sad, but she didn't let it deter her.

Instead, she prepared for the next mouse. She found a box, filled it with ripped paper towels and a sock, and decorated it with a few flowers. She even made a sign that said, "If you're not a mouse, KEEP OUT."

I admire her.

She doesn't give up. Just because one little mouse died, didn't mean she wouldn't try to help more. She wouldn't be deterred.

Isn't that a great attitude?

Do not be anxious about anything,
but in every situation, by prayer
and petition, with thanksgiving,
present your requests to God.
(Philippians 4:6 – NIV)

How often do we want to give up on praying for something because we don't feel God is answering our prayers? I know sometimes I feel like giving up. I bet you do, too.

But please don't. Your prayers matter. Sometimes, they're answered in ways we can't see or comprehend. But they're always answered.

I urge you, my friends, to keep praying. Pray for the little things, pray for the unlikely, and pray for the seemingly impossible.

And don't give up.

Reflections

What spoke to you the most from today's reading?

_____

_____

_____

_____

Turn your thoughts into a prayer:

_____

_____

_____

_____

Is the Holy Spirit prompting you to do anything in response?

_____

_____

_____

_____

Day 21

Have you ever had your mind feel like spaghetti? Where one strand of thought leads to another, which intersects with another and then takes a sharp turn to another, and everything goes around and around in one gooey mess?

It's easy for our minds to be busy. And in the age of phones and social media, our minds are constantly being trained to be distracted rather than focused.

And now, dear brothers and
sisters, one final thing.
Fix your thoughts on what is true,
and honorable, and right,
and pure, and lovely, and admirable.
Think about things that are
excellent and worthy of praise.
(Philippians 4:8 – NLT)

Our primary focus should always be on God and things that are good. But what about focusing on the task at hand?

Look straight ahead, and fix your
eyes on what lies before you.
(Proverbs 4:25 – NLT)

While this verse still pertains to keeping our focus on God in all things, I think it also contains good advice for us today.

Do one thing. Don't get distracted by what's on the right or the left. Focus on the task at hand and enjoy the moment to its fullest.

So, how exactly do we do that?

I think it takes practice.

Give it a try, and then try again. Eventually, you'll get the hang of it, and it'll be worth it.

Reflections

What spoke to you the most from today's reading?

_____

_____

_____

_____

Turn your thoughts into a prayer:

_____

_____

_____

_____

Is the Holy Spirit prompting you to do anything in response?

_____

_____

_____

_____

Day 22

I removed all my social media apps from my phone a while back. While I admit part of this had to do with privacy and tracing, part of it involved using my time more productively.

And it worked! Sort of...

I spend much less time on my phone, but let's be honest—I didn't really spend a ton of time on it before. Not like my kids—they're champs at using their phones.

However, I still gravitate towards my phone at various times throughout the day.

Currently, I only use it for messaging and a colouring app (and sometimes I play solitaire if I can't sleep).

The other day, my daughter and I were watching a show together, and she asked me if I had seen what happened.

And I hadn't.

Why? Because I was colouring on my phone and didn't look up in time!

I like the colouring app because it's calming, but I don't feel like I have time to use it throughout the day, so I 'multi-task' by doing it while I watch TV. It feels more productive that way.

But is it?

While it seems like the latest technology is creating a generation of successful multitaskers, the truth is that it's creating a generation that doesn't know how to focus or concentrate on the task at hand.

And what if that includes our time with God?

But Jesus often withdrew to
lonely places and prayed.
(Luke 5:16 – NIV)

Do you allow yourself to be distracted during Bible reading or prayer time? Does your phone ding and pull your mind away from what God is saying to you?

Then perhaps you'd be up for a challenge. What apps can you delete from your phone today to help you focus better on God and life around you? Pray about it and go where God leads you.

Reflections

What spoke to you the most from today's reading?

_____

_____

_____

_____

Turn your thoughts into a prayer:

_____

_____

_____

_____

Is the Holy Spirit prompting you to do anything in response?

_____

_____

_____

_____

Day 23

God created us with many different personalities. I'm grateful that we're not all the same, but sometimes, being different makes it difficult to communicate.

What people hear when I speak isn't always what I intended to say. And likewise, sometimes what I hear others say isn't what they meant.

One week, I had to deal with a couple of unfortunate circumstances caused by mis-communication. At least that time, I wasn't the one who miscommunicated, but I did get caught in the crossfire, so to speak.

Let me be clear at this point that neither of these situations was dire or significant. They were just nominal things.

Even so, my first reaction was to get upset and defend myself. I wanted to declare how it wasn't my fault and make sure no one thought ill of me.

Yet God impressed upon my heart to let it go.

He knows the truth. He knows what happened. And He knows my heart is innocent of wrongdoing (in these cases). And I should rest in that.

The Lord is my strength and my defense;
he has become my salvation.
He is my God, and I will praise him,
my father's God, and I will exalt him.
(Exodus 15:2 – NIV)

I don't need to defend myself – God is my defender.

And He's your defender, as well.

Hanging on to things we're meant to let go of only hurts us and hinders us from living in the current moment with God. It doesn't matter what others think of us. It only matters that we're living to please God.

Is there something you need to let go of today?

Trust Him. Rest in Him.

Be still.

Reflections

What spoke to you the most from today's reading?

_____

_____

_____

_____

Turn your thoughts into a prayer:

_____

_____

_____

_____

Is the Holy Spirit prompting you to do anything in response?

_____

_____

_____

_____

Day 24

I recall when a decision had to be made about my youngest's schooling. Should she continue receiving her education in a Christian school or return to homeschooling?

There were many pros and cons on both sides. The school was great, but with my oldest no longer attending and driving to school, the back and forth would equal 900 kilometres of driving for me each week!

Homeschooling had worked out great in the past, but I had plans to return to writing full-time that fall. Moreover, my youngest has a dire need to see friends all day, every day. So, there were downsides to choosing to homeschool again, as well.

Sometimes, decisions are black and white. One side doesn't align with Scripture and is more a matter of fighting our flesh, while the other is the Godly choice.

But as in this case, sometimes, neither decision is wrong. But what would be the best for her? What would God have us do?

Trust in the Lord with all your heart; do not depend on your own understanding. Seek his will in all you do, and he will show you which path to take.
(Proverbs 3:5-6 – NLT)

For weeks, we submitted our will to God, prayed like crazy, read Scripture, and talked it out.

As much as I often wish God would use a megaphone and shout instructions in my ear, that's not how He works.

Instead, it's always the whisper. The nudging of the heart.

Finally, we felt led to return to homeschooling.

Once the decision was made, I felt at peace. My daughter was excited, too! I even felt at peace about my writing schedule being cut in half. I knew it would still work out. God is in control.

So, do you struggle to hear God's voice?

Don't give up.

Keep seeking Him. Read His 'instruction book' daily - the Bible is full of the wisdom and direction we need to live.

Reflections

What spoke to you the most from today's reading?

_____

_____

_____

_____

Turn your thoughts into a prayer:

_____

_____

_____

_____

Is the Holy Spirit prompting you to do anything in response?

_____

_____

_____

_____

Day 25

When my office was still in my bedroom, I had three bird feeders hanging outside the window—a hummingbird feeder, a suet cage, and a shallow plate often filled with rainwater.

One morning, I sat at my desk and looked out the window before starting work. For about ten minutes, my kitties Cookie and Holly joined me as we thoroughly enjoyed a visit from a family of red-breasted nuthatches.

There was one adult, and two babies. Funny enough, the babies were larger than the adult! So, I could only presume the adult was the male since female birds are generally larger (male and female nuthatches have the same plumage).

I watched as the tiniest baby followed Dad to the suet feeder. Baby latched her feet onto the wire cage and flitted her wings while Dad picked off pieces and put them in Baby's mouth. Then, Baby would imitate Dad and try to get a piece or two by herself.

Next, Dad flew to the plate and took a sip of water. The baby followed and did the same thing.

Then it was bath time! Dad splashed in the

water, and Baby imitated his every move.

After that, Dad flew to the tree, and Baby followed him to the nearest branch beside him.

Can I just say it was the cutest thing ever?

Therefore be imitators of God,
as beloved children.
(Ephesians 5:1 – ESV)

There is no better way to learn than to watch and imitate the teacher.

To be Christ-like, we must spend time immersed in the Bible to see what kind of life He lives—and what a wonderful life it is. Why wouldn't we want to be like Him?

What can you do today that's Christ-like?

Reflections

What spoke to you the most from today's reading?

_____

_____

_____

_____

Turn your thoughts into a prayer:

_____

_____

_____

_____

Is the Holy Spirit prompting you to do anything in response?

_____

_____

_____

_____

Day 26

When I come home, my dog and four kitties come to greet me. I pet and snuggle each one, distinctly aware of how much time this takes, especially if all I did was go to the mailbox.

My daughter says you can't pet only two because then there's the worry the other three will feel left out. Therefore, you have to pet all five every time.

I don't disagree.

So, this begs the question. Are five pets too many? Can you have too many cats?

The more you have of something, the more time is required to attend to such things.

Have a pool? You need to invest time to treat it, clean it, and, of course, enjoy it.

How about a garden? How much time is needed to plant it? Tend it? Weed it? Harvest it?

None of these things are bad. They can all be quite pleasurable and add value to our lives.

But what is that time taking us away from?

Do we give up time with God because we have to run too many errands?

Do we forsake reading His word because there's too much to do today?

And, in those moments of pleasure, do we remember to be thankful or worship God alongside what we're doing? Remember the story of Martha and Mary in Luke:

But Martha was distracted with much serving. And she went up to him and said, "Lord, do you not care that my sister has left me to serve alone? Tell her then to help me." But the Lord answered her, "Martha, Martha, you are anxious and troubled about many things, but one thing is necessary. Mary has chosen the good portion, which will not be taken away from her."
(Luke 10:40-42 – ESV):

Martha wasn't doing a bad thing; it just wasn't the best thing for the moment.

May we examine our moments and ensure we're choosing the best thing.

Reflections

What spoke to you the most from today's reading?

_____

_____

_____

_____

Turn your thoughts into a prayer:

_____

_____

_____

_____

Is the Holy Spirit prompting you to do anything in response?

_____

_____

_____

_____

Day 27

Do you ever have those days where you feel completely overwhelmed? Some days I can look at my big to-do list and feel fine and excited about the tasks at hand, and other days they just feel like a big mountain. I really don't know what the difference is.

Well, sometimes I know. Sometimes, the mountain appears because I focus on the tasks instead of God. In that situation, I need to spend time with God and turn my eyes on Him. Then, things become clear.

But occasionally, that's not the case. I can spend time in The Word in the morning, and in prayer during a walk in the woods. I can ask God what to do each step of the way, yet still feel a little blue and overwhelmed.

And that's okay.

It's okay to have days with ups and downs, even if your attention is on God as it should be.

The bottom line is, He's still got me.

He's still got you.

The Lord himself goes before you and will be with you; he will never leave you nor forsake you. Do not be afraid; do not be discouraged.
(Deuteronomy 31:8 – NIV)

And that's the key. I can feel overwhelmed or a little sad, but He will see me through, so there's no need to feel afraid or discouraged.

So, be encouraged today.

He's there with you, right where you are.

Reflections

What spoke to you the most from today's reading?

_____

_____

_____

_____

Turn your thoughts into a prayer:

_____

_____

_____

_____

Is the Holy Spirit prompting you to do anything in response?

_____

_____

_____

_____

Day 28

It was such a tragedy when my beloved computer died.

No warning. Just crash. Complete darkness.

Thankfully, I had almost everything backed up. However, circumstances required me to order a new one online and wait two weeks for a computer.

Wow—what an eye-opener! I knew I was dependent on my computer for things, but I didn't realize how dependent I was.

I could still use my phone to check emails and messages, but writing, newsletters, bookkeeping, and other work were out.

It felt a bit like the Dark Ages. LOL.

On the other hand, I did a lot of reading and sorting through closets.

But the experience got me thinking.

What if I misplaced my Bible for two weeks? What if my Bible app crashed?

Would I feel as lost? Would I feel as panicky and out of sorts?

During my computer blackout, I spent more time than usual in the Word, which made me hungrier for more of Him.

May we all feel the need for God and reading His Word, as much as we feel the need for our computers.

And yes, I realize I use my computer for work, and I have things that need to be done, but shouldn't God be first and foremost in ALL things?

So, how about a little challenge?

For the next week, pick up your Bible and read for ten minutes every day. Just read. Ask God for clarity. Ask Him to draw you near.

Nothing is more fulfilling than God.

Draw near to God and He will
draw near to you.
(James 4:8 – NKJV)

Reflections

What spoke to you the most from today's reading?

_____

_____

_____

_____

Turn your thoughts into a prayer:

_____

_____

_____

_____

Is the Holy Spirit prompting you to do anything in response?

_____

_____

_____

_____

Day 29

I remember when friends adopted an adorable border collie, Australian shepherd, and hound mix. As with all puppies, it was adorable. One night, they brought it by to show my kids.

It's one thing to see a photo, but another to hold the warm, soft bundle of cuteness in your arms and feel the loving puppy kisses!

Of course, this quickly developed into a hankering for another new puppy for ourselves. How could it not?

But then I remembered what the first couple of years were like.

It's not all sleepy cuddles. There's training, and pooping, and training, and running, and training, and chewing... sigh. It's a lot of work!

But then I think of the dogs I've had. Once they got past that stage, they've all been such good dogs! Even with their little quirks.

I love the morning and evening walks, the cuddles, and the tail wags when they see their people.

And their great personalities.

We've loved every dog we've ever owned and wouldn't have traded them for the world.

And isn't that how God feels about us?

When we first come to Him, we're broken, untrained, and undisciplined.

But He works with us. He guides us. Teaches us. Loves us.

For I am convinced that neither death nor life, neither angels nor demons, neither the present nor the future, nor any powers, neither height nor depth, nor anything else in all creation, will be able to separate us from the love of God that is in Christ Jesus our Lord.
(Romans 8:38-39 – NIV)

He trains us up to be like Him.

And when we mess up (as we're always bound to do), He doesn't stop loving us or give us away.

He holds us tighter and helps us to do better next time.

Be encouraged today, and rest in His love.

He's got you!

Reflections

What spoke to you the most from today's reading?

_____

_____

_____

_____

Turn your thoughts into a prayer:

_____

_____

_____

_____

Is the Holy Spirit prompting you to do anything in response?

_____

_____

_____

_____

Day 30

With spring comes an abundance of rain, and the quiet little creek in our backwoods swells, making a large swath of the regular path unpassable. Numerous flooded areas extend up the banks, across the trail, and deep into the woods.

One spring, I tried going for a walk, and between trying to keep my footing on the remaining ice patches and not stepping in the huge puddles, it proved quite tricky.

In fact, I got a couple of ice-cold soakers along the way.

The next day, after even more rain, I decided to try again. This time, I remembered I owned a pair of rubber boots.

What a difference.

This time, feet adequately protected, I easily walked through the edges of the large puddles and bypassed them without much effort. My feet stayed warm and dry.

I was instantly reminded of the armour of God.

Therefore, put on every piece of God's armor so you will be able to resist the enemy in the time of evil. Then after the battle you will still be standing firm. Stand your ground, putting on the belt of truth and the body armor of God's righteousness. For shoes, put on the peace that comes from the Good News so that you will be fully prepared. In addition to all of these, hold up the shield of faith to stop the fiery arrows of the devil. Put on salvation as your helmet, and take the sword of the Spirit, which is the word of God. (Ephesians 6:13-18 – NLT)

Just like my boots, it's one thing to know about the armour – and another thing to put it on and use it against the enemy's schemes.

We want to be able to stand firm. Are you wearing your armour today?

Reflections

What spoke to you the most from today's reading?

_____

_____

_____

_____

Turn your thoughts into a prayer:

_____

_____

_____

_____

Is the Holy Spirit prompting you to do anything in response?

_____

_____

_____

_____

HAVE TEA WITH ME!

Thanks for reading God Moments! I hope and pray this devotional drew you closer to God. I'd love to spend more time with you. Join me for tea?

Tea With Wendy is a newsletter I send out to friends where I share photos, life stories, a God Moment, book news and other fun stuff.

And when you sign up, you'll get a few FREE GIFTS!

I'd love to see you there. Sign up at: wendyaddison.com/tea-with-wendy

READ OTHER BOOKS BY WENDY ADDISON:

DEVOTIONALS:

God Moments: First Steps – 10 Devotions to Awaken and Grow Your Faith (FREE at wendyaddison.com)

God Moments – Volume 1: 30 Devotions to Awaken and Grow Your Faith

God Moments – Volume 3: 30 Devotions to Awaken and Grow Your Faith (COMING SOON)

FAITH AND FOILS COZY MYSTERY SERIES:

Fishers of Menace

Apple of My Die (FREE short e-story)

Ablazing Grace

Peril of the Bells

Faith, Rope, and Love

Pray Without Deceasing

HELP AN AUTHOR OUT?

Could you spare a minute and please leave a review for *God Moments – Volume 2*? It's the best thing you can do for an author, next to buying the book.

It doesn't have to be long. Giving a rating and writing a simple sentence will do. And you can simply copy and paste the same review to other sites. No need to write a new one. Thanks so much!

Here are suggestions for where you could leave a review:

Goodreads

Bookbub

Amazon

Your favourite online retailer

ABOUT THE AUTHOR

Meet bestselling author Wendy Addison, the creative mind behind soul-stirring devotionals that weave together faith, humour, and heartfelt insights to awaken your faith and enrich your spiritual growth.

Wendy's faith-driven journey is marked by a profound commitment to living out Christ's teachings through both personal and professional pursuits. Over the years, she has worked in children and youth ministry, directed a Christian theatre company, volunteered with international outreach organizations, and led Bible study groups. Her mission work and birdwatching adventures have taken her to nearly twenty countries, enriching her appreciation for God's creation—though spiders remain a challenge.

Wendy now resides nestled amidst the whispering trees of her 26-acre Canadian woodland retreat. She has four wonderful children, a fluffy dog, and mischievous feline companions who are always ready to lend a paw—or distract her with their antics.

So, wrap yourself in a cozy blanket with a steaming mug of tea and dive into Wendy's devotionals for a meaningful time filled with inspiration and warmth.

Sign up for the *Tea With* Wendy for regular updates, stories and new God Moments from Wendy, at: wendyaddison.com/tea-with-wendy

FOLLOW WENDY:

BookBub: @WendyAddisonAuthor

Goodreads: Wendy Addison

Facebook: Wendy Addison – Author

Instagram: @wendyaddisonauthor

Web: wendyaddison.com